ACHIEVING FINANCIAL FREEDOM IN YOUR 20'S.

SERIES:

FINANCIAL FREEDOM AT ANY AGE.

ACHIEVING FINANCIAL FREEDOM IN YOUR 20'S

Series "Financial Freedom at Any Age"
By: D.K. Hawkins
Version 1.1 ~October 2021
Published by D.K. Hawkins at KDP
Copyright ©2021 by D.K. Hawkins. All rights reserved.

No part of this publication may be reproduced, distributed or transmitted in any form or by any means including photocopying, recording or other electronic or mechanical methods or by any information storage or retrieval system without the prior written permission of the publishers, except in the case of very brief quotations embodied in critical reviews and certain other noncommercial uses permitted by copyright law.

All rights reserved, including the right of reproduction in whole or in part in any form.

All information in this book has been carefully researched and checked for factual accuracy. However, the author and publisher make no warranty, express or implied, that the information contained herein is appropriate for every individual, situation, or purpose and assume no responsibility for errors or omissions.

The reader assumes the risk and full responsibility for all actions. The author will not be held responsible for any loss or damage, whether consequential, incidental, special, or otherwise, that may result from the information presented in this book.

All images are free for use or purchased from stock photo sites or royalty-free for commercial use. I have relied on my own observations as well as many different sources for this book, and I have done my best to check facts and give credit where it is due. In the event that any material is used without proper permission, please contact me so that the oversight can be corrected

The information provided in this book is for informational purposes only and is not intended to be a source of advice or credit analysis with respect to the material presented. The information and/or documents contained in this book do not constitute legal or financial advice and should never be used without first consulting with a financial professional to determine what may be best for your individual needs.

The publisher and the author do not make any guarantee or other promise as to any results that may be obtained from using the content of this book. You should never make any investment decision without first consulting with your own financial advisor and conducting your own research and due diligence. To the maximum extent permitted by law, the publisher and the author disclaim any and all liability in the event any information, commentary, analysis, opinions, advice and/or recommendations contained in this book prove to be inaccurate, incomplete or unreliable, or result in any investment or other losses.

Content contained or made available through this book is not intended to and does not constitute legal advice or investment advice and no attorney-client relationship is formed. The publisher and the author are providing this book and its contents on an "as is" basis. Your use of the information in this book is at your own risk.

TABLE OF CONTENTS.

TABLE OF CONTENTS. 4

INTRODUCTION 6

CHAPTER 1. 11

    In Your Twenties, Is It Possible To Earn Six-Figure Income? 11

CHAPTER 2. 15

    What Is The Secret To Financial Freedom? 15

CHAPTER 3. 21

    What Are Your Financial Goals For The Long Term? 21

CHAPTER 4. 27

    How to Modify Your Ideas and Behaviors. 27

CHAPTER 5. 34

    Use the 80/20 Rule for Your Finances. 34

CHAPTER 6. 38

    Adopt The Financial Success Formula. 38

CHAPTER 7. 44

    Financial Resolutions for Investing. 44

CHAPTER 8. 51

    A Home-Based Business Is Your Best Option For Financial Freedom. 51

CHAPTER 9. 55

Re-Wire Your Mindset for Success to Hit a 7-Figure Income. 55

CONCLUSION. 60

INTRODUCTION.

Whether you are in your twenties, have begun your professional career in the corporate world, and have a steady source of income, one question will constantly dominate your mind: "Do you need a financial plan?" You're probably asking why you need it if your grandparents or parents didn't.

The answer to all the above concerns is that you need a financial strategy if you have goals, as lifestyles were drastically different 20-30 years ago. The world has shifted dramatically, as have our lifestyles. We now have additional methods to spend our money.

This feeling of financial independence has worn off. Now is the time to figure out how to manage your money in a way that ensures your financial security during your career and into retirement. After all, you'd like to see your goal of turning your small change into a large sum of money become a truth.

As we all know, human wants are infinite and limitless. They will evolve during our lives. To achieve these needs/objectives, we must arrange for financing, which may be accomplished by 'income creation' through employment or savings/investments.

Financial planning is a systematic way to generate the funds necessary to accomplish our goals. In the simplest terms, financial planning is achieving life goals stated in monetary terms through prudent financial management.

It is a systematic technique in which the financial planner maximizes the client's existing financial resources by utilizing the most appropriate financial planning tools and investment vehicles to accomplish the client's financial goals and objectives.

It is one of the things that few people consider. However, it is important to do so since it can make our lives easier because we cannot foretell the future. Therefore, if we begin planning our financial future today, we can see the manifestation of our financial ambitions.

Financial planning is the most relevant and client-centered method available in financial consulting. It is the most practical method of allocating cash flows to the many life goals of an individual. Therefore, purchase a property, a car, or take a vacation. Whatever goals you have in mind, financial planning can help you achieve them.

Financial planning's mission is to ensure that an investor has the appropriate quantity of money available to him at the appropriate moment to enable him to accomplish various life goals.

Every individual who earns money should plan, which may appear to be a daunting responsibility. Thus, a competent financial planner is required to assist you in maintaining your financial independence.

Time never stands still. As you age, your needs and those of your family will change. Also, the context in which you find yourself will change. New investing opportunities will arise. Some previous investments may no longer make sense or will need updating over time.

A person in their twenties will have distinct demands as they enter their thirties. Having a financial plan is important but not sufficient if you wish to live a relatively stress-free life in the future.

The above debate boils down to that you should begin financial planning in your early twenties. There is no better time than your twenties to start putting your money to work for you, giving your life direction, and assisting you in achieving your life goals. I will provide you with reasons to engage in financial planning that will help you navigate through all periods of life.

By forming sound spending and saving habits in your twenties and saving money for the things that matter to you, you will undoubtedly build sizable nest eggs that you may use in the event of an emergency and during retirement.

The old proverb, "A penny saved is a penny earned," will apply to you if you practice sound financial planning and saving. Financial planning also provides guidance, the direction you need to make intelligent financial decisions, ensuring that you avoid costly mistakes and reap the advantages for the remainder of your life.

Thus, as the proverb goes, "the rich man plans for tomorrow, the poor man plans for now"; therefore, begin planning for tomorrow like a rich man and avoid being a pauper.

Happy Reading

CHAPTER 1.

In Your Twenties, Is It Possible To Earn Six-Figure Income?

There is no longer a standard method of earning money in this world. People of our parents' generation were more inclined to believe that you should get a solid job by attending university and working your way up the career ladder. This will enable you to finally earn enough money to ensure a more likely future saved for retirement than enjoyed in your twenties.

The key to earning a high income that exceeds the six and seven-figure mark is to leverage the power of the Internet.

A recession-proof business where millions of people discover that a world of wealth is waiting for them by earning money online. The freedom and lifestyle that comes with owning their own highly automated business is the selling point for so many young entrepreneurs in their twenties who want to enjoy life without being tied to a desk in their 9 to 5 jobs.

Thus, how are these young aspirants earning money, and is it secure?

There are many different ways to earn money online. Some are quite effective for novices, while others are less effective and are better suited to the more experienced Internet Marketer. The top four internet money-making opportunities fall under the following categories:

1. Affiliate marketing.

2. Data entry and questionnaires.

3. Multi-Level Marketing (MLM) or Network Marketing.

4. Direct Sales.

Affiliate marketing is the practice of selling another person's products in exchange for a small commission, often around $30. Therefore, if you do the math, you'll discover that earning a considerable income needs a high volume of purchases; this is why it works best when you already have a sizable subscriber list and should be viewed as a supplement to your primary income.

You'd have to work extremely hard to earn six and seven figures selling other people's stuff, and as they say in our company, it's all about working smarter, not harder. Data input and surveys are not the best ways to attain your financial goals; you are effectively exchanging your time for money, they are somewhat monotonous, and you may even come across frauds that waste your time but do not pay you!

Many people who look for work at home opportunities online will surely pursue MLM or Direct Sales opportunities. This method generates massive income for Internet Marketers worldwide, and it is where most success stories are found.

The disadvantage of MLM marketing is that your revenue is not always guaranteed, as when people in your upline or downline quit the firm, this certainly affects your income.

Direct sales, particularly of high ticket products that pay significant commissions of $1000 to $2000 directly into your bank account, is the preferred method of Internet Marketers seeking financial independence. This path is not dependent on your team, and it is possible to earn large sums of money very rapidly, even if you do not have an extensive subscriber list.

CHAPTER 2.

What Is The Secret To Financial Freedom?

The fundamental formula for financial success is straightforward: spend less than you make and invest the remainder. Also, continuously reinvest revenue increases.

It appears to be so straightforward, but why are most people poor?

Perhaps they are unsure about how and where to invest prudently?

Or is it because no one has advised them to save?

That is not the case. We've all heard some money-saving strategies but were disappointed when we tried them, another theory that is completely inapplicable in my work. Also, how can I save money if I just have enough money to cover my next salary?

Whatever we earn, the quantity of money remaining at the end of the month reflects our capacity to grow our capital. Indeed, this is all we have earned, and others have earned everything we have spent. You may disagree, but the important value is the sum of your acquired capital, less your debt.

If you believe that what you earn is "reasonable," but after liabilities, just a small amount of capital remains, then someone else is successfully using your earned money.

Which is more valuable: well-paid employment or starting your own business?

Should you continue working for someone else or start your own business? It is entirely dependent on your unique circumstances and, while we're on the subject of income, there are two types: active and passive. Active income is earned when you are compensated for your labor time. If you work, you will receive. If you do not labor, you will receive nothing.

Passive income is earned when your time and effort are repaid multiple times. For instance, the author completed a novel within two years. However, the book became a success, and he will receive income for many years due to his two-year commitment.

Also, investing creates passive income. If you invest your active income prudently, you can establish a source of passive income. Your own business can also generate passive income, but only if you establish a business system that operates independently of your direct intervention.

Most individuals who start a business do so to establish a career for themselves. They are not employed. Their company employs them. Also, remember that 80 percent of small firms fail during the first five years of operation.

For those who do not see a long-term future in hired labor, are unwilling to assume significant risk, or lack creative business ideas, there is the option of connecting to established company systems such as network marketing.

This is another method, open to anyone, of generating a passive income stream. You only need to find a reputable organization with a track record of accomplishment and an excellent educational structure that enables you to learn from leaders, not from average academics.

Why is there such an emphasis on passive income? Because they can set you free.

What does it mean to "liberate" you? The phrase "liberty" has a plethora of definitions. My preferred definition of liberty is as follows: Liberty = time Plus money. If you have enough time but not enough money, you cannot pick what to do or where to go. If you have money but lack the necessary time, you are still not free.

Financial liberty is the only path to true liberty. Financial independence is attained when your passive income enables you to live the lifestyle you wish. Then you can work only when and as much as you wish. Isn't that incredible?

The issue is that it appears impractical to most people. This is a result of a lack of self-discipline on our part. It appears to be a self-service restaurant in life: Everyone now at the head of the line was formerly at the tail end.

Most people change lines often, typically before they reach the middle of the queue. They will never make it to the front line, where the most delectable pastries are packed.

The prerequisite for financial success is straightforward. The sooner you establish habits for capital growth, the sooner you will reap the benefits of financial success.

Where to begin?

One of the reasons most individuals do not become wealthy is that they lack a clear concept of what constitutes an asset. That is, they lack a clearly defined objective. Recognize that it is extremely difficult to accomplish something about which you are unsure. As a result, you should begin with your long-term goals.

CHAPTER 3.

What Are Your Financial Goals For The Long Term?

It is important to respond clearly to this question, as our most powerful computer, the subconscious mind, cannot comprehend numbers. It needs a clear visual representation. No wonder Donald Trump, the famed multimillionaire, stated, "If my imagination can envision it clearly, it must be possible to do."

Before pursuing long-term ambitions, each individual should handle their financial security. Financial stability is contingent upon two factors: life and disability insurance and the accumulation of a "financial buffer."

What is meant by the term "financial buffer"? This is the amount of money held safely that is required to support your family's essential costs for 6-

24 months if you lose your source(s) of income unexpectedly.

Everyone believes, "It will never happen to me," but it often does. Also, consider how much more at ease a person feels when he knows that, if necessary, he will have sufficient time to locate another job or even change careers entirely. You must keep this money unused and cannot gamble with it.

It is not advisable to retain these funds in a bank account or a safe deposit box at home. Life and disability insurance, of course, are important to protect people closest to you. That should be your first financial objective.

Is saving a viable way of self-enrichment if a person saves only a portion of his income?

After ensuring financial security, you can decide how to increase your capital. The first choice to make is how much of your money you will pay yourself. That is, what percentage of your monthly salary you will save. However, there is an issue. How am I to determine how much money I will retain each month? Because financial conditions change month to month and sometimes there is nothing left over.

The answer is simple: pay yourself first when you receive a paycheck! That means that as soon as earnings arrive in your account, you should deposit a portion of them into a dedicated savings account.

That alone is insufficient, as most individuals cannot resist the temptation to spend the money, and their discipline is violated. They do not pay themselves because they believe they will save twice as much the following month. The next month, history repeats itself, and finally, individuals feel powerless to carry out this aspect of their plan.

To circumvent this, you must automate this process. For instance, if you receive your pay on the tenth of each month, establish an automated transfer to your savings account on the eleventh.

Consider what would happen if a 19-year-old young guy set aside $250 US each month for himself.

Each year, he would save $3000 US! Please guess how much wealth he will accumulate as a 65-year-old if he does not utilize the money until he reaches that age and puts it in financial assets that provide an average annual return of 10%?

The answer is $1.5 million in the United States. The result is usually remarkable because compound interest kicks in when you save money each month and invest it.

If you are unfamiliar with investing, you can contact your bank's manager of investment product marketing. Choose a manager who will not attack you by recommending one or another fund without clarifying your long-term investment objectives.

A good manager should assist you in developing an investment strategy that is tailored to your specific objectives and personal qualities, such as risk tolerance. Regrettably, management in most banks nowadays behaves like average salespeople. They have a product and are looking for ways to sell it.

This is not, however, a justification to forego saving. It is not worthwhile to expedite the procedure. Take your time and concentrate on locating the perfect specialist, focused on your specific needs as a client.

To summarize:

1. Determine how much of your earnings you will pay yourself.

2. Take care of yourself first. Following that, compensate others.

3. Automate the process.

Does this suggest that, in most cases, each individual can progressively become wealthy?

If I had to summarize everything, I would say that most people never get wealthy because they do not structure their lives like a business that must generate profit at the end of each year.

We did not investigate specific skill-intensive capital-raising tactics, such as active trading on a stock exchange, option trading, or other methods. This chapter focused primarily on ideas and habits, which are responsible for and may change.

After a few behaviors are changed, we will gain access to larger sums of money. Also, we will be prepared for new difficulties, and when a pupil is ready, the teacher will always appear!

CHAPTER 4.

How to Modify Your Ideas and Behaviors.

Adults in their twenties are confronted with extraordinary personal problems. In a position to make our own choices, we are often paralyzed by dread and uncertainty.

However, if they are willing to modify their ideas and behaviors, all "twenty-somethings" have the opportunity to carve out a healthy, happy, and independent life. This entails living deliberately rather than passively waiting for someone else to determine the next step.

1) Be yourself.

There are no exceptions. Attend to the sense of knowing that exists within you and act on its behalf. There are individuals, locations, and occupations that will bring you to life. Your objective is to maximize them in the service of your passions.

When the knowledge within you fills you with joy, there truly is no better feeling in the world. Consider living with that level of freedom, comfort, and aliveness daily.

How wonderful would that be?

What kind of life could you lead?

2) Assume financial accountability.

Determine how much money you will earn and when. You should be aware of how much money you spend and on what.

Are they in sync?

With a single online search, there are many free and simple strategies to balance your budget.

Fear of financial distress does not change reality; it merely paralyzes you into inaction and creates additional issues. Knowing what you own and owe enables you to make prudent financial decisions.

3) Extracurricular activities are not optional!

Play is a necessary component of living a healthy and happy life. Everyone needs and deserves time for relaxation and enjoyment. Whether you perform in the mountains, on the beach, at the theater, or even at a neighborhood coffee shop. The important thing is to get out there and play.

The on-ramp to job success directs a significant portion (dare I say all?) of our attention into work-related activities, professionalism, maturity, and continuing learning.

That is all good, but being your best self does not need a 24-hour-a-day commitment to work.

Often, it is our downtime that provides us with the most fulfilling hours. We all contribute something helpful to the world; if we do it from a place of enjoyment, we may improve our contribution.

4) Assemble a "Joint."

As a twenty-something, the chances are you're in a new location or experiencing the same place in a new way. While it can be tempting to wait for opportunities to present themselves, nothing may be more likely to result in misery.

Assemble your new life actively; become a "joiner." Identify a group of people who will miss you if you are cannot be present. Begin by pursuing your interest. If you can join a career-related group, it would be fantastic. If a leisure-time organization calls your name, that's fantastic. The most effective approach to secure happiness is to work on its behalf! Do it.

5) Broaden your Horizons

When things aren't going well, change your perspective. Change your mindset—how is this an opportunity? Is it possible for me to change my attitude? One thing is some: if you repeatedly tell the same sob tale to yourself, your friends, or your family, you might convince yourself that this is the only way to view the situation.

To be honest, there are millions of additional perspectives available, but you may have to take a significant step backward to get them. The world will do what it pleases. It is preferable to broaden your acceptable range, maximizing your capacity for adjustment, than to confine your happiness to periods when everything is as you like.

6) Take Chances.

I am not advocating for reckless, short-term gain at the expense of long-term suffering hazards.

What risks are you willing to take?

Take those on your behalf for the sake of your desire.

What is your PASSION in life?

Find a method to include it in your daily routine. There will never be a day when you have fewer duties than you do now.

Accept some risks early in life; do not wait until you are burned out to resurrect your goal. Defend your passions and dreams. Prepare financially, socially, and emotionally for your risk-taking. Assure yourself of the support you'll need to go for it and live largely.

7) Remember that today is your day.

Everything in your life occurs due to your permission - from the most unsettling credit card bills to the less-than-ideal apartment to the friend who moans at every opportunity. Every day, you create your universe via your thoughts, words, and actions. "I took this soul-sucking 40/60/80-hour-a-week job to protect myself from starving" is no way to get up each morning.

"I have landed a stable employment that will enable me to pay off my debts and achieve financial freedom by the time I reach the age of 26" fosters a more constructive environment and opens the door to further excellent opportunities. This optimism enables you to focus on future goals, passions, and desires.

You are the creator of your universe; ensure that it is the world you desire.

What are you enduring and why?

What would be different if you were willing to confront these issues?

What could be the source of your happiness?

We all deserve happiness. What is your first move in making it a reality for you?

CHAPTER 5.

Use the 80/20 Rule for Your Finances.

Popularly known as the Pareto principle, the 80 20 rule is perhaps one of the most prominent financial management strategies that allow people to focus on the important things and get more things done.

In productivity words, this rule asserts that 80 percent of your entire results should come from only twenty percent of your labor. It also means that eighty percent of your effort impacts just twenty percent of your ultimate results. So how can you implement the rule for personal financial freedom?

Everybody has a different set of circumstances. Everybody lives a distinct lifestyle, and practically everybody has their spending patterns. Therefore using the 80 20 rule in your scenario could be extremely different from the people around you.

Suppose we are trying to work on a personal budget to get financial freedom. In that case, the primary area of concentration should be the areas within your expenditure that demonstrate the highest spending.

This collection of expenses would normally be your eighty percent. The fact is that more often than not, we are told to make cuts in the region of daily expenditure like lunches and coffee, but in truth, these are things that will save you pennies, and they usually sit inside your twenty percent range.

The main categories of personal expenditure and the eighty percent region generally include housing expenditures, running a vehicle or two, and personal debt. Before implementing the 80 20 rule, you should analyze these significant expense categories to determine any immediate solutions to cut the spending back.

One example would be to consider taking on a roommate, as this would significantly cut spending on housing. In some circumstances, you may lower your housing payments or rent to half of what you currently spend.

Another thing you could consider is carpooling. This concept has existed for a long period. Many people in previous generations insisted on traveling in this fashion to and from work.

It will help you save money on petrol, tolls and parking expenses. Also, you might request that everybody traveling with you contribute to the vehicle's costs by giving money each time they ride in your automobile.

Personal debt is often one of the largest areas of expenditure. You will enjoy significant gains if you can pay off your debt in full or pay down huge quantities as they become available. This will help save money on interest payments and help you pay off debt faster than the initial loan agreement specified.

Double-check your agreement beforehand if you plan to do this, as some loans include an early repayment condition. Occasionally, a penalty fee will be assessed for paying off debt ahead of the scheduled payment period.

Essentially, if you can apply the 80/20 rule to your budget and daily expenses, you will discover that financial independence is not difficult to attain. It will need some forethought and persistence. This will ensure that you do everything possible to avoid incurring unnecessary costs.

CHAPTER 6.

Adopt The Financial Success Formula.

Why do some people attract wealth like a magnet, while others are destined to earn a middle-class income or live paycheck to paycheck regardless of their efforts?

According to the world's wealthiest people, financial success is determined by human ideas and attitudes to a degree of up to 80%. In comparison, knowledge and abilities on generating money accounts for only 20%. While it would be a misconception to suppose knowledge is useless in this scenario, people do not generate money purely based on what they know.

Money-related destructive thoughts such as "no money wins" or "honest means did not earn money" lurk in our subconscious and impede us from having the best possibility of acquiring further funds. Though we are often unaware, we follow those beliefs and receive the results because our beliefs and thoughts directly affect us.

Thus, what makes you wealthy?

Thomas J. Stanley performed a survey of 733 multimillionaires and interviewed them. The study asked respondents to identify the top 30 characteristics that, in their opinion, contributed most to their success.

To summarize the statistics, the first five most important factors were as follows (the percentage of respondents who named each item is indicated in brackets):

1. Consideration for others (57 percent).

2. Self-control (57 percent).

3. Capacity to reach an agreement with others (56 percent).

4. A partner who empathizes with and supports you (49 percent).

5. Capacity to work more diligently than others (47 percent).

Some people may be wondering at this point: "Nonsense - success is contingent on different factors. You'll need an initial monetary investment, wealthy family and contacts, and it's even advantageous to be able to climb over other individuals '". If you believe that, I have some bad news for you! You are one of those individuals who feel the formula for success is "To Have. To Make. To Be."

Perhaps you're thinking to yourself, "If I had initial funds, prominent friends, and sound ideas, I would start a firm, invest, create or patent something, and I would be content (rich, successful, loved, etc.). However, I lack all of it, which is why I am not as successful as I would like to be." What is wrong with this picture? To be sure, your formula is inverted.

In truth, the opposite is true: you must first develop self-confidence, responsibility, ambition, and tenacity and act (create, grow, take chances, move on, etc.) to achieve high performance, success, affluence, and recognition.

There is one straightforward technique to maintain your current capacity for attracting and retaining money:

1. Begin by calculating your current capital (immovable and moveable assets, cash accounts, and securities);

2. Subtract all existing debts (loans, leasing, and so on) from the total amount you have;

3. Divide the total by the no. of years you have worked gainfully;

4. Subtract the result from 12.

The resulting number is a true indication of the average amount of money you've earned per month thus far. The remainder of your earnings has been divided among others (restaurants, shops, travel agencies, banks, petrol stations, etc.).

Individuals often lament their inability to earn a living. Are employers truly underpaying?

Are you familiar with the sensation or thinking that you would have more money if your employer just increased your pay?

However, a rise in compensation is not required or necessary. Why?

According to this law, because most people adhere to Parkinson's Law, "Costs increase until they equal income." The first prerequisite for financial success is to cultivate the habit of continuously violating Parkinson's Law.

How long have you been an employee?

How many times have they boosted your wage throughout this period?

How near were you to financial independence during that period?

Or perhaps you've relocated? Perhaps as your income increased, your debts increased as well?

Perhaps you're being squeezed in ways you've never been squeezed before?

Perhaps you're hesitant to "rock the boat" or take bold actions since you can't afford to reduce your income even temporarily because banks and leasing firms are knocking at your door?

If this describes your position, then your employers are not at fault for paying you insufficiently. It is solely due to your behaviors that you have been sucked into the "hamster wheel." You must keep this wheel spinning continuously because if it stops for even a split second, your entire life will implode like a house of cards.

CHAPTER 7.

Financial Resolutions for Investing.

If you've been making resolutions since you were nine years old or if this is your first year, I have some suggestions beyond the standard "get healthier" and "get organized."

In 2021, the third most popular New Year resolution is to increase savings and decrease spending. I'm sure those who drafted this resolution had the best of intentions. Being more precise, on the other hand, brings in superior results. To get you started, here are five suggestions:

1. This year, save more money than you did last year.

This resolution, second only to becoming healthy, has the potential to have the most significant impact on your life. There are many aspects of this world over which you have no control. Everyday, "secure" employment is lost.

Each year, stock markets experience ups and downs. Each week, a "significant" sale is lost. If you spend your time attempting to change things you cannot control, you will have an extremely frustrating life.

You have complete control over how much money you save. Whether or not you've begun saving for a home, retirement, or a dream vacation, there is always more money to save. If you saved nothing last year, make 2021 the year you begin saving $50 every month. If you are already a diligent saver, this is the year to ramp up your savings.

This has been a resolution of mine for the last two years. I've gone from saving nothing to approximately $1000 every month. I'm putting money down for a new car, a new house, vacation, and retirement. I'm not saying this to brag; I'm saying it to demonstrate that it is achievable.

How am I to pull this off?

I do this through technology (which we shall discuss in a moment) and an accountability partner. Setting reminders and automating withdrawals from my bank account compels me to save, and having a friend who constantly reminds me is a benefit in disguise. If you need an accountability partner, don't hesitate to get in touch with me. I would be delighted to assist.

2. Pay off one of your loans.

Debt is a pain. Paying off debt is even more unpleasant. Unfortunately, debt levels for early 20-somethings range from $12,000 to $78,000 for 28 and 29-year-olds. If you are in your early twenties, begin repaying debt immediately before it gets unmanageable. If you are in your late twenties, commit to paying off your debt before reaching the ripe old age of thirty.

This is an excellent resolution since you can make it as difficult as you like. Perhaps you have a $500 credit card balance from Christmas shopping. You can pay off that bad boy and cross this resolution off your list in a matter of days.

If you're looking for a more difficult challenge, perhaps you have a $10,000 student loan. Making a strategy to pay off $833.33 per month to eliminate your student loan debt by the end of 2016 will make you feel like a victor. Not to mention how amazing it will feel after it is paid off.

I recommend that you examine your financial situation and choose a debt that is both feasible and significant. Determine the monthly payment required to reduce debt and adhere to it.

Many credit card providers and bill collectors will allow you to set up an automatic monthly repeating payment. Make a note of it and forget about it. Then, when 2016 arrives, you'll be one loan payment closer to financial independence.

3. Establish or amend your budget

I'm a firm believer in budgets. I believe that everyone, even the ultra-wealthy, should have a budget. Budgets compel you to ascertain your financial situation, your spending capacity, and your priorities.

If you adore going out on Friday evenings, by all means, create a budget category devoted to Friday nights. If you aspire to acquire a new Lexus, create a budget category dubbed the Lexus fund.

If you lack a budget, make 2021 the year you give it a try. I guarantee you'll feel more secure about your finances and future and have more fun than you did last year. If you are a seasoned budgeter, review it to determine if any of your objectives have shifted.

I'm aware that my budget for nights out with pals was reduced last year to save for a larger vacation. I had a fantastic time on vacation last year, and I didn't miss anything significant by missing a few Friday nights with my friends.

4. Utilize technology to assist you in achieving your financial goals

We consider ourselves fortunate to be the first generation to be entirely digitally proficient. We understand how to use the internet effectively and efficiently to improve (simplify?) our lives. Apps have become ingrained in our daily lives (try finding somewhere without Google maps). It's past time for our finances to catch up to the rest of our technological lives.

Whatever your financial objectives, technology can assist you. Personal Capital or Mint are budgeting tools that can help you in creating or modifying your budget. Investing programs like Robin Hood, Wealthfront, Betterment, or My Pathway can assist you in making future investments. Not to mention the vast network of financial consultants eager to help Generation X&Y.

Utilize your phone for purposes other than Facebook, Snapchat, and the latest game, and you may find yourself a bit wealthier next year.

5. Acquaint yourself with the fundamentals of investing

If you've completed the preceding steps, the next best step is to acquire or improve your investing knowledge. In its simplest form, investing is the process through which you use your money to generate other funds.

Investing can be as sophisticated or as simple as you like. To my mind, you should never invest in anything that a ten-year-old cannot comprehend. Whatever direction your investments go, begin with the fundamentals.

CHAPTER 8.

A Home-Based Business Is Your Best Option For Financial Freedom.

To be sure, most of us wish to have more money in our life. Typically, this entails taking on a second job or establishing our own business.

I've concluded that a viable home-based company model is the way to go, particularly with low start-up costs, low operating expenses, and low overhead costs. Now we must choose the type of business/company to establish and the product or service to market.

Consider the following: we offer health, diet, and nutrition supplements, discounted medical and dental plans, discounted legal/lawyer services, cosmetics, and candles, as well as virtually everything else in between.

The great majority of these organizations that sell these products and services typically need you to construct a list of friends and relatives, host "home parties" or meetings, make numerous cold calls, and develop a massive network of distributors beneath you.

Let us examine the preceding scenario. The most prevalent MLM home-based business model is the sale of health and nutrition items. Hey, I'm all for maintaining a healthy and active lifestyle, and nutritional supplements should be a part of everyone's daily routine.

The issue with most MLM organizations that advertise these products is the high cost/price and the hype and big claims made about their "latest and greatest" miraculous supplement...whether it's a diet pill, powder, potion, or some wonder drink.

While these are highly consumable products, you ask individuals to alter their lifestyles to obtain something they require but may not necessarily desire. This can be fairly challenging, especially when comparing products of comparable quality that can be acquired at a significantly lower price elsewhere.

They are also riddled with complications concerning the various items and services mentioned above and the organizations that promote them. Either they sound fantastic in principle and on paper but fall short in practice and may come with some strings attached.

The primary issue here is that changing people's behaviors is extremely tough, compounded by most people despising selling "things" and bugging their friends and family.

The perfect home-based business opportunity should have affordable startup expenses, allow you to conduct most of your business from home (typically over the internet), eliminate the need to phone hundreds of people, pester your family and friends, and eliminate the need to store/stock inventory of products.

It should be a product or service that people WANT and desire, not just NEED. People are constantly seeking knowledge to assist them in resolving a problem or issue in their lives. What is one item that everyone wishes they had more of?

Money is the most obvious option. A product that equips people with the tools and knowledge necessary to succeed in marketing, the lifeblood of every organization, is a precious commodity.

Another critical consideration is the compensation plan. You want a compensation plan that rewards handsomely for each transaction. Forget about those Mickey Mouse compensation programs that pay you $5, $10, or $20 per transaction. That is simply insufficient.

To earn a living, you need to generate a large number of sales. You want a compensation scheme that swiftly results in profit. After all, our time is precious and limited.

CHAPTER 9.

Re-Wire Your Mindset for Success to Hit a 7-Figure Income.

It's no secret that leads are crucial to your business, but what good is even three hundred leads every day if you're not mentally equipped for success?

If you have a poverty mentality and lack the leadership qualities required to handle yourself on the phone, it doesn't matter how many leads you're contacting because NONE of them will join you!

Now I know the "mindset" concept isn't sexy. Everyone would much rather study the newest and greatest marketing strategies to have leads flowing in regularly but leads mean absolutely NOTHING if your mind isn't right.

So how can you get your thoughts right?

What are top income earners doing with their mind to quickly and readily bring in an endless quantity of money to their businesses when ninety percent of the people in this field make less than ten dollars per week?

Let's go into this ever-so-important topic because this is the most vital element of the entire process of becoming a successful entrepreneur, and this is the ONLY reason why people fail.

Your mind is the most powerful thing in the world you can tap into. It can be your greatest ally that serves you and delivers everything you need to create a life without limits. It can be your worst enemy, always attracting difficulties, pain and difficulty into your existence. Your mind is who you will have the most discussions with within this lifetime, and YOU get to select what kind of connection you have with it.

Understand that you have a total of one-hundred percent control of your conscious thoughts. Yup, it's that powerful! This is tremendously significant because your conscious ideas daily will mold your subconscious mind, which is a force that you and I can't even completely fathom.

Whether you're awake or sleeping and whether you're aware of it or not, your subconscious mind is always working in concert with the world to deliver you what your conscious thoughts are focusing on.

It is your obligation to watch your thoughts like a hawk. As an entrepreneur, you cannot afford to focus on any lack, negativity, or worry, even more, if you are just getting started in this business and are broke because you will attract more of the same. This will destroy you and your business even before you begin.

You are not an employee, and you must shed that employee mentality. Suppose you want to get the results you desire in life. In that case, you must begin thinking like a successful entrepreneur, which you can accomplish by regularly plugging into training material that empowers you, helps you overcome self-doubt, and encourages you to imagine bigger.

Every second of the day, your thoughts are either bringing you closer to or further away from your goals. Life is either forward or backward; there is no in-between.

Successful millionaires in our field realize this and have spent years refining their thinking. They have conquered all self-doubt. They have honed their leadership skills. They are perpetually in a state of flow, which is rather lovely.

Top earners attract the resources necessary to pursue their objectives and goals. They attract these things through their subconscious minds, which they control consciously through conscious thought.

Consider your subconscious as a completely blank slate that will take whatever thoughts fed to it by your conscious consciousness. Your subconscious will work tirelessly and connect with the world to manifest your conscious thoughts, and it never fails.

The best news is that you can undoubtedly attain the outcomes and goals you desire in the same method that the top earners did! Work on your thinking, which is easier said than done, needs years of study, practice, perseverance, and hard work. Also, it is necessary if you want to achieve financial independence in your lifetime!

To develop a daily habit of constantly working on your mind, changing and rewiring your mindset for success, developing your Millionaire Mindset. You do this by joining a mastermind, continually feeding your brain positive thoughts, and being aware of the types of thoughts you're feeding your subconscious every second of every day.

This is a brutal fight to win on your own. Indeed, every great entrepreneur would credit a mastermind group or set of mentors for assisting them in molding their minds, which is directly accountable for their success. How many leads you generate; will fail without this component if your mind is not tuned in. If you're a needy individual, this is the only explanation.

CONCLUSION.

Why do some individuals work hard their entire lives and remain financially insecure (poor) when they should be relaxing in financial freedom? Is it because they were not born to make it, are incapable of thinking for themselves, or lack the rudiments of financial intelligence?

Financial intelligence or financial literacy is a gradual process of learning how to manage your money so that you may live debt-free and attain financial comfort, if not freedom, regardless of how little you make. In other words, financial literacy is the capacity to read numbers and comprehend the dynamics and operations of money.

In any society, achieving financial success is mostly a matter of attitude. In other words, it is determined by a person's attitude toward time, referred to as "time perspective."

Individuals who achieved financial success generally possessed a long-term view. They organized their daily, weekly, and monthly activities with the long term in mind. They considered the future five, 10, and twenty years in advance. They allocated resources and made judgments based on their impact on their desired state many years from now.

On the other side, those that are financially unsuccessful typically have short time horizons. They paid scant attention to the long term. They valued rapid gratification over long-term achievement and accomplishment. They were more focused on short-term enjoyment. As a result of this approach, individuals took short-term decisions that resulted in long-term difficulties.

Another reason many people struggle with financial insecurity is their propensity for minding other people's business rather than their own. Many people work hard at their job (as workers) merely to receive a paycheck (which provides them with a false sense of security). Still, others work extremely hard at their business and financial development to meet future financial issues as they arise.

A proverb states that "if you work hard at your job, you will earn a living, and if you work hard on yourself, you will earn a fortune." Thus, it is preferable to work harder on yourself and accumulate beautiful fortune than to work hard at your job and earn a stipend.

In other words, one cannot labor and hope to gain financial independence. Therefore, you must be able to think creatively, particularly in financial and money management.

Financial literacy is based on three fundamental financial values:

- Security
- Capacity for comfort
- Wealth/liberty.

Before we can consider financial freedom, we need a plan that provides the basic security for food, clothing, and housing and makes us comfortable (enables us to buy other comforts of life).

The good news is that becoming wealthy is automatic if you have a sound plan and adhere to it by acquiring and applying the necessary knowledge. Financial freedom/wealth achieved via prudent financial planning does not occur overnight; it happens over time.

Regardless of what you learn, there is always a strong association between financial understanding and the quality of financial planning. Your mindset will always be that the more knowledge you have, the wealthier you will become when acquiring wealth. On the other hand, ignorance continues to cost you money.

Regrettably, in today's jet era, everyone seeks a quick fix for their money difficulties. Nobody desires delayed satisfaction, which is a necessary component of true long-term riches.

Avoid being naive in believing that your financial difficulties would be resolved if you get a better job (which is highly unlikely) or a quick fix solution that does not exist. You must go through the proper steps to comprehend your financial status.

Thus, it is never too late for anyone interested in expanding their financial knowledge and skills to achieve financial independence. It is important to your financial future.

Thanks for Reading

Series: Financial Freedom at Any Age

1. Achieving Financial Freedom in your 20's
2. Achieving Financial Freedom in your 30's
3. Achieving Financial Freedom in your 40's
4. Achieving Financial Freedom in your 50's
5. Achieving Financial Freedom in your 60's
6. Achieving Financial Freedom in your 70's and beyond.
7. Achieving Financial Freedom in children
8. Achieving Financial Freedom in teenagers
9. Achieving Financial Freedom in college students.